HOW I RESPOND

A Workbook to Track and Change How You
Respond to Things to Which You Often React

CHRISTOPHER L. SMITH

DEDICATION

This workbook is dedicated to all those people who have wanted and who do want to shift from reacting to life around them to truly responding.

INTRODUCTION

Too often in life we simply react to what goes on around us. Something happens and we simply react to it. At times, this can get us in trouble because our reaction is too quick, too strong or off in some other way. When this happens, it can wreak havoc in our lives.

Learning to respond rather than react involves becoming aware of what goes on in our interactions. Looking at things that are underlying what we do and then intentionally working to change our behaviors can lead to a much more peaceful way of going through our days.

Having a therapist or counselor can be helpful in order to talk about what is going on, to help point out things that might be going on under the surface and to encourage alternative ways of responding. This book is not meant to be a substitute for such guidance, in fact this book can be helpful for recording what is going on so that you and your therapist or counselor can more clearly work with what is going on. Our memories of events can get fuzzy so writing things down at the time can really help.

Even if you do not have a therapist or counselor, going through the exercise of recording what is going on and thinking about it can be helpful. This book gives you the opportunity to do just this. For each event complete the log that spans two pages. On each log, you will be asked about what took place, your thoughts and feelings about it, how you reacted/responded, the result and any changes you would make next time. As you do so, watch for patterns and see if you are able to move more to responses over time.

As Viktor E. Frankl (a great thinker in therapy as well as a survivor of Nazi Germany):

❝ Between stimulus and response there is space.
In that space is our power to choose our response.
In our response lies our growth and freedom.

May your growth and freedom lead you to wholeness and peace.

Think about the types of situations to which you have been worried about how you respond. Think also about your responses and how you have been impacted by them. Write down some of your thoughts.

_____

_____

_____

_____

_____

_____

_____

_____

_____

_____

_____

_____

_____

_____

_____

_____

_____

What happened:

_____
_____
_____
_____
_____
_____
_____
_____

How I interpreted what happened:	Objectively what was going on or could have been going on:

How what happened and what I thought made
me feel:

_____
_____
_____
_____
_____

What I did (or decided | How it turned out:
to do):

_____|_____
_____|_____
_____|_____
_____|_____
_____|_____

What I learned from all of this:

_____
_____
_____
_____
_____

What happened:

_____
_____
_____
_____
_____
_____
_____
_____
_____

How I interpreted what happened:	Objectively what was going on or could have been going on:

How what happened and what I thought made me feel:

What I did (or decided to do):

How it turned out:

What I learned from all of this:

What happened:

_____

_____

_____

_____

_____

_____

_____

_____

How I interpreted what happened:	Objectively what was going on or could have been going on:

How what happened and what I thought made me feel:

_____

_____

_____

_____

What I did (or decided to do):	How it turned out:

What I learned from all of this:

_____

_____

_____

_____

What happened:

_____

_____

_____

_____

_____

_____

_____

_____

How I interpreted what happened:	Objectively what was going on or could have been going on:

How what happened and what I thought made me feel:

_____

_____

_____

_____

What I did (or decided to do):	How it turned out:

What I learned from all of this:

_____

_____

_____

_____

What happened:

_____

_____

_____

_____

_____

_____

_____

How I interpreted what happened:	Objectively what was going on or could have been going on:

How what happened and what I thought made me feel:

_____

_____

_____

_____

What I did (or decided to do):	How it turned out:

What I learned from all of this:

_____

_____

_____

_____

What happened:

_____

_____

_____

_____

_____

_____

_____

How I interpreted what happened:	Objectively what was going on or could have been going on:

How what happened and what I thought made me feel:

_____

_____

_____

_____

What I did (or decided to do):	How it turned out:

What I learned from all of this:

_____

_____

_____

_____

What happened:

_____

_____

_____

_____

_____

_____

_____

_____

How I interpreted what happened:	Objectively what was going on or could have been going on:

How what happened and what I thought made me feel:

What I did (or decided to do): | How it turned out:

What I learned from all of this:

What happened:

_____

_____

_____

_____

_____

_____

_____

How I interpreted what happened:	Objectively what was going on or could have been going on:

How what happened and what I thought made me feel:

What I did (or decided to do):	How it turned out:

What I learned from all of this:

What happened:

_____

_____

_____

_____

_____

_____

_____

_____

How I interpreted what happened:	Objectively what was going on or could have been going on:

How what happened and what I thought made me feel:

_____

_____

_____

_____

What I did (or decided to do):	How it turned out:

What I learned from all of this:

_____

_____

_____

_____

What happened:

_____

_____

_____

_____

_____

_____

_____

_____

How I interpreted what happened:	Objectively what was going on or could have been going on:

How what happened and what I thought made me feel:

_____

_____

_____

_____

What I did (or decided to do):	How it turned out:

What I learned from all of this:

_____

_____

_____

_____

What happened:

_____

_____

_____

_____

_____

_____

_____

How I interpreted what happened:	Objectively what was going on or could have been going on:

How what happened and what I thought made me feel:

_____

_____

_____

_____

What I did (or decided to do):	How it turned out:

What I learned from all of this:

_____

_____

_____

_____

What happened:

_____

_____

_____

_____

_____

_____

_____

_____

How I interpreted what happened:	Objectively what was going on or could have been going on:

How what happened and what I thought made me feel:

_____

_____

_____

_____

_____

What I did (or decided to do):	How it turned out:

What I learned from all of this:

_____

_____

_____

_____

_____

What happened:

_____

_____

_____

_____

_____

_____

_____

_____

How I interpreted what happened:	Objectively what was going on or could have been going on:

How what happened and what I thought made me feel:

_____

_____

_____

_____

_____

What I did (or decided to do):	How it turned out:

What I learned from all of this:

_____

_____

_____

_____

What happened:

_____

_____

_____

_____

_____

_____

How I interpreted what happened:	Objectively what was going on or could have been going on:

How what happened and what I thought made me feel:

_____
_____
_____
_____

What I did (or decided to do):	How it turned out:

What I learned from all of this:

_____
_____
_____
_____

What happened:

_____

_____

_____

_____

_____

_____

_____

_____

_____

How I interpreted what happened:	Objectively what was going on or could have been going on:

How what happened and what I thought made me feel:

_____

_____

_____

_____

What I did (or decided to do):	How it turned out:

What I learned from all of this:

_____

_____

_____

_____

What happened:

How I interpreted what happened:	Objectively what was going on or could have been going on:

How what happened and what I thought made me feel:

What I did (or decided to do): | How it turned out:

What I learned from all of this:

What happened:

_____

_____

_____

_____

_____

_____

_____

How I interpreted what happened:	Objectively what was going on or could have been going on:

How what happened and what I thought made me feel:

What I did (or decided to do): | How it turned out:

What I learned from all of this:

What happened:

_____
_____
_____
_____
_____
_____
_____
_____

How I interpreted what happened:	Objectively what was going on or could have been going on:

How what happened and what I thought made me feel:

_____

_____

_____

_____

What I did (or decided to do):	How it turned out:

What I learned from all of this:

_____

_____

_____

_____

What happened:

_____

_____

_____

_____

_____

_____

_____

_____

How I interpreted what happened:	Objectively what was going on or could have been going on:

How what happened and what I thought made me feel:

What I did (or decided to do):	How it turned out:

What I learned from all of this:

What happened:

_____

_____

_____

_____

_____

_____

_____

_____

How I interpreted what happened:	Objectively what was going on or could have been going on:

How what happened and what I thought made me feel:

What I did (or decided to do):

How it turned out:

What I learned from all of this:

What happened:

_____

_____

_____

_____

_____

_____

_____

_____

How I interpreted what happened:	Objectively what was going on or could have been going on:

How what happened and what I thought made me feel:

_____

_____

_____

_____

What I did (or decided to do):	How it turned out:

What I learned from all of this:

_____

_____

_____

_____

What happened:

_____

_____

_____

_____

_____

_____

_____

_____

How I interpreted what happened:	Objectively what was going on or could have been going on:

How what happened and what I thought made
me feel:

What I did (or decided | How it turned out:
to do):

What I learned from all of this:

What happened:

_____

_____

_____

_____

_____

_____

_____

How I interpreted what happened:	Objectively what was going on or could have been going on:

How what happened and what I thought made me feel:

What I did (or decided to do):	How it turned out:

What I learned from all of this:

What happened:

_____

_____

_____

_____

_____

_____

_____

_____

How I interpreted what happened:	Objectively what was going on or could have been going on:

How what happened and what I thought made me feel:

_____
_____
_____
_____

What I did (or decided to do):	How it turned out:

What I learned from all of this:

_____
_____
_____
_____

What happened:

How I interpreted what happened:	Objectively what was going on or could have been going on:

How what happened and what I thought made me feel:

What I did (or decided to do):	How it turned out:

What I learned from all of this:

CONCLUSIONS

By now, you should have a better understanding of how and why you react. You may have ideas of what will help you to stop reacting and start responding. As you work on this, you will realize that you are developing better control over your life. Hopefully, with this you will be experiencing more wholeness and peace (or shalom) in your life.

You really are in charge of how things around you influence you and what it does inside of you. In the words of the Dalai Lama, remember:

❝ Don't let behavior of others destroy your inner peace.

If you are still having difficulty with how you are reacting, you might want to find a counselor or therapist that you can trust and sit down with them. They have methods that can help you explore what is going on and look at alternatives.

ABOUT THE AUTHOR

Of course, in the truest sense of the word, you and those part of your journey are the author of this journal. However, the framework has been created and produced for you by the one listed as the author, Christopher L. Smith.

Christopher has been involved in a diverse range of areas in his training and experience. His approach through life is not to treat these as distinct dimensions, but rather to see the connections across various dimensions. This book blends together his training in pastoral counseling that began at Yale Divinity School with the organizational structures learned studying operations research.

His own work with clients, at the time of preparing this resource, was through Seeking Shalom (www.SeekingShalom.org), a teaching practice in New York and Indiana of which he is the founder and clinical director, where clinicians intentionally incorporate spirituality into the therapeutic process. His professional life has also included service as the chair of the Presbyterian Serious Mental Illness Network and as the president of the American College of Counselors, as well as regional and local leadership roles. He is licensed as a marriage and family therapist, mental health counselor and clinical addictions counselor. His therapeutic work includes working with individuals, couples, families and groups around a variety of clinical issues.

In addition to this resource, Christopher has authored a number of other resources and books. If you are interested in learning more about his writings, please look him up at http://AnAuthor.com/Christopher.

www.ingramcontent.com/pod-product-compliance
Lightning Source LLC
Chambersburg PA
CBHW071640040426
42452CB00009B/1714